The Essential Writer's Notebook

A STEP-BY-STEP GUIDE TO BETTER WRITING

Written and illustrated by

Natalie Goldberg

PETER PAUPER PRESS, INC.
WHITE PLAINS, NEW YORK

For my mom,
Sylvia Edelstein Goldberg,
who told me I could do anything

■ ■ ■

The text in this notebook has been reprinted from the following sources:

WILD MIND: LIVING THE WRITER'S LIFE by Natalie Goldberg,
copyright © 1990 by Natalie Goldberg.
Used by permission of Bantam Books, a division of Random House, Inc.

LONG QUIET HIGHWAY by Natalie Goldberg,
copyright © 1993 by Natalie Goldberg.
Used by permission of Bantam Books, a division of Random House, Inc.

THUNDER AND LIGHTNING by Natalie Goldberg,
copyright © 2000 by Natalie Goldberg.
Used by permission of Bantam Books, a division of Random House, Inc.

Designed by Lesley Ehlers

Illustrations copyright © 2001 Natalie Goldberg

Published July, 2001 by
Peter Pauper Press, Inc.
202 Mamaroneck Avenue
White Plains, NY 10601
All rights reserved
ISBN 0-88088-243-3
Printed in Hong Kong

Visit us at www.peterpauper.com

INTRODUCTION

THE ESSENTIAL WRITER'S NOTEBOOK is a place where you keep your hand moving, even if you think you have nothing to say. Stop your daydreaming; put pen to paper. Trust yourself. Write whatever is on your mind. Write what you see, taste, feel. Write about what's in front of your face—the man with a red nose and bushy black hair and a dachshund on a leash; the way he keeps his left hand at his waist and guides the dog with the right. The spruce by the curb, the red Pontiac that drives by. It is a November afternoon and the world is almost dull except that you notice and record it. That single act makes it alive and wakes you up.

In this notebook you are free to *practice*—you don't have to begin the great American novel or write like Toni Morrison, Hemingway, or Virginia Woolf. This is the place to meet your own gritty mind—to learn how you think and to write how that first kiss felt, how that last pear tasted, who you were in the summer of 1987.

Tell the truth: winter is your favorite season, you never liked avocados, and you're afraid to swim. Record the honest details of your life—not how you think you should be, but how you are. What do you remember about the old house you lived in, the bike you left behind, the café on the corner where you ate croissants and sipped Earl Grey? What great mistake have you made in your life?

Who are your angels, and how did you betray yourself? What has been the best love of your life, and what has brought you to your knees?

Write the essentials. Don't forget Aunt Pearl and Cousin Max, the ratty calico across the way that Uncle Joe sneaked into the house to lap at cream in the orange saucer. Where were you when Martin Luther King was shot? Maybe that was too long ago—how about when the First Lady became a senator?

Nothing you write is too much. Let it out. Write everything you know about trucks, Oreos, ginkgo trees, palms, goldfish, mashed potatoes, Paris, France. Don't forget to throw in the color red, an old shoe, a cucumber, a mouse, a rickety chair, and a heavy cloud. Where have you traveled? It can be to Zimbabwe or Cleveland—it doesn't matter; tell us the details. What is your dentist like, your auto mechanic, the florist, the grocer?

What is more essential than your feet, your hands, a candy bar, yesterday's dream? Pay tribute to all the everyday and extraordinary things. Everything's essential; every thing belongs in the pages of this notebook.

N. G.

Chair. France, 1997

KEEP YOUR HAND MOVING. When you sit down to write, whether it's for ten minutes or an hour, once you begin, don't stop.

What is the purpose of this? Most of the time when we write, we mix up the editor and creator. Imagine your writing hand as the creator and the other hand as the editor. Now bring your two hands together and lock your fingers. This is what happens when we write.

If you keep your creator hand moving, the editor can't catch up with it and lock it. It gets to write out what it wants. "Keep your hand moving" strengthens the creator and gives little space for the editor to jump in.

Keeping your hand moving is the main structure for writing practice.

LOSE CONTROL. Say what you want to say. Don't worry if it's correct, polite, appropriate. Just let it rip.

BE SPECIFIC. Not car, but Cadillac. Not fruit, but apple. Not bird, but wren.

Don't chastise yourself as you are writing. Just gently note that you wrote "tree," drop to a deeper level, and next to "tree" write "sycamore." Don't give room for the hard grip of the editor.

Ruth & Jimmie's, Mississippi, 1996

DON'T THINK. We usually live in the realm of second or third thoughts, thoughts on thoughts, rather than in the realm of first thoughts, the real way we flash on something. Stay with the first flash. Writing practice will help you contact first thoughts. Just practice and forget everything else.

DON'T WORRY ABOUT PUNCTUATION, SPELLING, GRAMMAR.

GO FOR THE JUGULAR. If something scary comes up, go for it. That's where the energy is. Otherwise, you'll spend all your time writing around whatever makes you nervous. It will probably be abstract, bland writing because you're avoiding the truth.

Carson McCullers House, Nyack, NY, 2000

DO A TIMED WRITING FOR TEN MINUTES. Begin it with "I remember" and keep going. Every time you get stuck and feel you have nothing to say, write "I remember" again and keep going. To begin with "I remember" does not mean you have to write only about your past. Once you get going, you follow your own mind where it takes you. You can fall into one memory of your mother's teeth for ten minutes of writing or you can list lots of short memories.

NOW TRY "I'M THINKING OF" FOR TEN MINUTES. Then, "I'm not thinking of" for ten minutes. Write, beginning with "I know," then "I don't know," for ten minutes. The list is endless: "I am, I'm not;" "I want, I don't want;" "I feel, I don't feel."

ONE OF THE RULES OF WRITING PRACTICE IS, DON'T THINK. We want to get below discursive thought to the place where mind—not your mind or my mind but mind itself—is original, fresh. It's not *you* thinking. Thoughts just arise impersonally from the bottom of our minds. That is the nature of mind—it creates thoughts. It creates them without our controlling them or thinking them. If you don't believe me, try to sit comfortably and still without thoughts for five minutes and just watch your breath coming in and out of your nose. I bet you can't do it. Writing practice lets the thoughts, visions, emotions run through us and puts them on the page. Writing is the crack through which you can crawl into a bigger world, into your wild mind.

Looking Down from Third Floor at MOMA,
New York, 1999

OKAY, YOU SIT DOWN to make the list of things you want to write about and suddenly you can't think of one thing that interests you. That is because you are thinking on the level of discursive thought, like a water bug swimming on the surface of the water. It goes like this: "Ah, there's nothing to write about. I wonder when Jim will call. I have nothing to say." You yawn. You notice a No Smoking sign in the corner of the restaurant you're sitting in. What you have to do is drop to a deeper level, the level of your heart and breath, in order to make your list and you have to keep your hand going.

Drink a full glass of water continuously and slowly without taking the glass away from your lips. Watch your breathing as you drink. Watch how your mouth fills with water before it swallows. Feel your swallow. Look down through the glass. Keep drinking. Finish the whole glass. Now put down the glass, take your pen and list five to ten clear subjects to write about. Number one can be "how I swallow." Number two can be "plastic glasses." Then "my hand," "my arm," "rivers," "where I love water," "summer and ice cubes," "feeling cold on my lips." Get it? Go.

Take a slow walk down the block, I mean *slow* and meandering, to mimic the way you want your mind to be—dreamy—in order to drop below monkey mind. If you find yourself still obsessing about your baby-sitter, your husband, your diet, as you look in store windows, then walk slower. Feel your foot lift to step forward, feel your toes bending your boot. Or choose a color: red. Now walk around the block and notice where red is on your walk: the stop sign, the boy's sock, the tail light on the blue Chevy. After you finish walking, list every place you saw red. Now make the list of things you want to write about.

I SAY KEEP YOUR WRITING IN NOTEBOOKS rather than on separate sheets of paper or in looseleaf binders because you are less likely to tear out, throw out, or lose those written pages. Keeping in one notebook the good and bad writing—no, don't even think *good* and *bad*; think instead of writing where you were present or not, present and connected to your words and thoughts—is another chance to allow all kinds of writing to exist side by side, as though your notebook were Big Mind accepting it all. When you reread a notebook and it has all of your writing, then you have a better chance to study your mind, to observe its ups and downs, as if the notebook were a graph.

WE NEED TO LEARN TO ACCEPT OUR MINDS. Believe me, for writing, it is all we have. What does Natalie Goldberg think? The truth is I'm boring some of the time. I even think about rulers, wood desks, algebra problems. I wonder why my mother gave me tuna fish every day for lunch in high school. Then zoom, like a bright cardinal on a gray sky, something brilliant flashes through my mind, and for a moment I'm turned upside down. Just for a moment, then the sky is gray again for another half hour or a day or eight pages of writing in my notebook.

Hotel,
Antibes, France, 1997

BUT HOW IN OUR BUSY LIVES do we get any writing done in the first place? Often, at the moment a student begins to say, "But I have a full-time, demanding job, a family"—I cut her off: "S-T-R-U-C-T-U-R-E. *Structure your time.*"

OPEN THOSE DATE BOOKS that Americans are so fond of and schedule in writing time. If you have a busy week, don't beat yourself up for not being able to write every day. Look at your calendar. If next week you can fit in only a half hour for writing on Tuesday from ten to ten-thirty in the morning, good. Mark it down. Do you have another window of time? For how long? Let's push it further—where will you write? At the Blue Moon Café? OK, you've made a date, and like any other—with the dentist, the accountant, the hairdresser—you have to keep it.

LET'S TALK ABOUT THE SWEETHEART, that person we're going to develop and give form to inside, whose only job is positive thought.

"Nat, I'm proud of you. You wrote for three hours this morning," says the sweetheart.

"Naa, she sat at her desk for three hours. Put it all together, she wrote for an hour. She daydreamed the rest of the time." The editor or critic moves in to counteract the sweetheart.

The sweetheart retaliates. "Pay the editor no mind right now. She's a sourpuss. Believe me, if you write only one page a day, that's three hundred and sixty-five pages a year. That's a novel," responds the sweetheart.

WRITE FOR TEN MINUTES, GIVING THE SWEETHEART A VOICE. It's a mother, a grandfather, a teacher, whoever was a positive force in your life. Give that sweetheart power, muscle, courage, but don't make him or her belligerent, wasting time scrapping with the editor. The sweetheart has skillful means and wisdom, and knows that to fight with the editor is to get her hands stuck in tar.

Banana Tree, Florida, August, 1998

BUT I DON'T BELIEVE THE SWEETHEART when she tells me good things, you say. Well, start practicing believing, even if you don't believe. Go ahead. Take in that compliment even if it's gonna kill you.

We've been conditioned to respond to negativity. The editor says, "You are a bad writer," and we believe her. There's no such thing as a bad writer. There is just a writer sitting at her desk practicing, putting down her thoughts and memories, visions, stories, and impressions.

KEEP GOING. You're doing fine. Don't cross out. Don't think.

QUESTIONS THAT EACH PERSON WANTING TO WRITE should eventually be able to answer:

What's important to you?

What are the subjects that pull you?

What are you willing to be witness to—to stay in there and carry for a long time?

What are you the most afraid to write about?

What is your darkness?

Whom do you write for?

TRY THIS:

Take a discipline you know well, maybe running, tea ceremony, baking, painting. Try that first and then launch into timed writings. The other skill might warm you up for writing as long as it is about concentration. Concentration does not mean squeezing your brain tight, but rather relaxing it and bypassing the editor. You become so intent on what you are doing, the internal censor can't get a word in edgewise.

Runners, run first, then write.

Writers, write first, then run.

Then try the opposite. Experiment.

YEHUDA AMICHAI, AN ISRAELI POET, wrote about a bank teller he used to see at the bank, how she moved to Italy to go to medical school. After I heard that poem, I thought, "You have to be dumb to write. You even have to notice and care about a bank teller." It was a beautiful poem.

Get dumb. Don't take things for granted. When I told some New Yorkers about dumbness in a workshop two months ago, they were so relieved. They were tired of being alert and intelligent. They wanted dream time.

Walk around your neighborhood dumb for a half hour. Then go write about what you saw. Be specific. Stay with details.

Try this:

Sit down with the plan to write something you have always wanted to write but have never managed to get around to. This time, though, you are not timing yourself. You are sitting down with the determination to write it through, even if it takes all afternoon or night. Relax and ease into it. Promise yourself you'll burn through, put the real stuff down, and not get in your own way. You might have a few false, nervous starts. Okay, now, just go. Forget the starts, move further in. You'll fix the start later or you'll find out the true beginning is two pages into your writing. Just stay put and keep going for as long as it takes.

Antibes, France Goldberg 197

Untitled, Antibes, France, 1997

HAVE WAKING DAYDREAMS. Begin with "I am" and write in the present tense. Just let it roll out of you without thinking. "I am walking on the moon. Half my body is green and the other half is orange. The orange side has a story to tell, but I can't hear it." Dream writing is good practice in losing control.

TRY THIS:

Tell us what you do for everyone and not just for yourself. Go for twenty minutes. Be specific. Be brave. How are you a large person?

WATCH YOUR USE OF THE WORD *BECAUSE*. Writers don't need to explain things. They need to state them. "Not the why but the what." For example, I went to the store because I needed something. *Because* is not necessary in the sentence. Instead: I went to the store. I needed something. You don't have to link sentences up and make reasons for them. The juxtaposition speaks for itself. Don't get bogged down in the need to explain. Just state it as it is and be fearless.

BE CAREFUL OF THE USE OF THE WORD *VERY*. Usually we don't need it. It's a word that emphasizes something that has already been stated. "The boy was *very* timid." It doesn't add that much; and, as a matter of fact, "The boy was timid" gives us a more direct statement. We hear *timid* better without the hoopla of *very*. *Very* lessens the presence of the word it is modifying. "It is very good." Take out *very*. "It is good." This is a brave statement and is rarely used. Simple, direct, to the point. No doilies of lace *verys* are put around the quality of good. Just *good*.

IT IS THE SAME WITH THE WORD *REALLY*. "It was *really* fine." It almost sounds as though the writer doesn't believe it was fine—"Really, I promise, it was fine." "It was fine" is a simple, direct statement that you can stand behind. We don't have to fluff it up. Words and sentence structure reflect the integrity of a writer. State clearly what you have to say. Don't be afraid. Step forward.

Dawn on the Hudson, Nyack, New York, 1999

TRY THIS:

Write about something you loved, a time when you felt whole and complete in an activity all for itself. It could be something as simple as learning to make a grilled cheese sandwich, or the time your uncle taught you to tie your shoelaces into a bow. Something you concentrated on as a kid because the ability to concentrate is where the bliss and love come from. Be specific but don't forget to throw in a detail about a cloud out the window as you bent to tie the shoe. While you concentrate and narrow in, you are also aware of the whole world.

STUDENTS OFTEN ASK, "What do you need to do in order to become a writer?"

My reply is always the same, "Read, especially in your genre, listen deeply and, of course, write."

Why are so many people surprised by this answer? If we asked a coach, "How do you become a basketball player?" we'd expect him to reply, "Know the game inside out, study players, stay in good shape, practice."

It is the same with writing.

"BUT WHAT BOOKS?" my students ask. "What do you like? What are you reading?"

I tell them to become friends with a bookstore or library, hang out in it and peruse the shelves.

LITERATURE GIVES US THE GREAT GIFT OF THE PRESENT MOMENT. As we read we enter the author's mind and follow it like a train on its tracks. If the author derails—gets lost—so do we. But if she is alive, steaming along in her full power, we chug along with her deep into pleasure country. The writer is concentrating—she has been practicing a lot—and we get the benefit. Mind reflects mind. If we read someone who is awake, it helps to wake us up.

TRY THIS:

Make contact with a writer you know about. If she lives in your town, perhaps call her up and tell her you would like to take her to lunch. In a small town, it might work. In a city, she'll think you're crazy. Okay. Go to a workshop this writer is teaching, meet her on her own ground but don't try to impress her—just support her.

MAKE CONTACT WITH OTHER WRITERS. Go to workshops to meet people. Don't stay isolated. Make an effort to seek out people who love writing and make friends with them. It helps to confirm your writing life.

Salon de Thé,
Aix-en-Provence, France, 1997

I ADVISE STUDENTS to do only writing practice for two years to get in touch with their wild minds—to discover their true longings and fears. It's a strong foundation for writing; something you can rely on and go back to over and over.

Often the students balk—two years? But I'm taking this time to write—I have to prove myself. I have to publish, do meaningful work. I can't just fill notebooks.

Would you expect to play Wimbledon your first week ever on the court? I ask them. Trust me, this practice will make you strong.

Write every day for ten days in a row. Do not reread anything you have written for those ten days until two weeks later.

Then sit down in a comfortable chair and have a soft heart and read with interest and compassion what you have written. Underline sentences that stand out. Use those sentences as first lines for future writing practice. Put parentheses around sections you like. Develop those sections, if you want, not by reworking them but by using them again with more timed writing practice.

SOMETIMES WE HAVE A RAW, REAL ROOT THOUGHT from the bottom of our mind—"I am going to die someday"—and instead of staying with that and feeling our fear or curiosity, we grab that thought and try to choke it. "No, not me. Let's not think about that. I'd like to buy a red car instead of a blue car." These are second and third thoughts. In writing we want to stay with first thoughts, that raw energy that comes from the bottom of the mind. In order to do that, we must embrace the whole mind, be mind-full.

Worth Avenue,
Palm Beach, Florida, 1999

WHEN YOU DO WRITING PRACTICE, sometimes you get high, feel happy and whole for the rest of the day, and you don't know why. It is because you contacted first thoughts, before they became fettered with second and third thoughts. You stayed with the real grit of your mind.

NOW AFTER TWO YEARS OF WRITING PRACTICE we've opened our minds, and they're huge fields with pintos and stallions running wild. Ahh, very good; we can take the next step. It is time to bridle that stampede, pick up the reins and slowly take control of that power.

Now begin an "I remember" exercise but stay only with memories of 1986 or fifth grade or that lunch in Manhattan with Polly last August—that one specific meal at one specific place with one person. Accustom your wild mind to taking direction.

HERE IS A GOOD EXERCISE: imagine a scene as a photograph—the moment a husband tells his wife he's just been fired from his job—and describe what you see. You cannot say, "She was shocked and furious." You cannot say, "She was sympathetic." These are not pictures. We are trying to bring the scene vividly alive in the reader's mind. Instead, focus on the face of the woman in the photo: her lower lip is curled, ringed hand stretched out toward the man across the couch, eyes narrowed in slits. What does he look like? What are they wearing? And the room? Flowered carpet? Fern in the corner? Stay with what is given. The reader will glimpse the feelings far more immediately in the gesture—the curled lip, the outstretched arm—than in any abstract statement. Here we are developing writing as a visual art, using our eyes as the primary way into a scene.

RAYMOND CARVER SAID IN *FIRES* that once he had the first sentence of a short story, he made the rest of the story as he made a poem: "one line and then the next, and the next."

Now find a sentence you like that comes from you. Don't be picky with your mind; instead, feel the sentence's integrity with your body. It can be a simple line. "I fell in love with my life one Tuesday in August." Now go ahead and lay down the next line and the next. Don't think further ahead than the next line. Don't think back. Just build that story.

Let the structure of the story unfold, one sentence after another.

WAKE UP TO EVERYTHING.

We can't use what someone else had—a great teacher, a terrific childhood. That is outside ourselves. And we can't avoid an inch of our own experience. Our job as writers is to wake up to everything.

ABOUT THE AUTHOR

NATALIE GOLDBERG lives in northern New Mexico. She is the author of several books on writing—*Writing Down the Bones, Wild Mind, Thunder and Lightning*—as well as a chronicle of a journey of awakening, inspired by her study of Zen Buddhism *(Long Quiet Highway),* and a novel, *Banana Rose.* More of Natalie's paintings can be viewed in her book *Living Color: A Writer Paints Her World.*

Natalie teaches writing in workshops nationwide. For more information on writing workshops and painting exhibitions, please visit her website at www.nataliegoldberg.com.